What to do when your mom or dad says ...
CLEAN YOUR ROOM

By
JOY WILT BERRY

Living Skills Press
Fallbrook, California

Distributed by:

Word, Incorporated
4800 W. Waco Drive
Waco, TX 76710

Dear Parents,

CLEAN YOUR ROOM! You've probably said that more than once to your child and received a less than enthusiastic response. Has it ever occurred to you that your child's resistance to your request may come from not knowing **how** to do what you have asked? Assuming that a child will automatically know how to fulfill a request is often the cause of much parent-child conflict.

If you expect your child to do something that he or she is not equipped to do, it is most likely that your child will become overwhelmed and anxious while you become frustrated. Both reactions are prime conditions for a knock-down-drag-out fight.

Why not avoid these kinds of encounters? Who needs them? Much of the negative "back and forth" that goes on between you and your child could be avoided if both of you approached your expectations intelligently.

Fulfilling **any** expectation always begins with knowing how. Skills are required to do any task, no matter what the task may be. These skills must be learned **before** the task can be accomplished. This is a fact of life!

All too often parents have left their children to discover these skills on their own through trial and error over a very long period of time. Why? You wouldn't give your child a complicated book in the beginning and say, "Teach yourself to read."

My suspicion is that most parents do not teach their children the skills needed to accomplish everyday tasks because they themselves do not know the skills and therefore do not know **what** to teach their child.

Does this apply to you? If it does, relax! The Survival Series for Kids not only helps children survive the demands of everyday living, but helps parents survive as well.

If you will take the time to go through the Survival Series with your child, both of you will learn some very valuable skills ... skills that will really pay off in the long run.

Some children will be able to read the books and assimilate all the information themselves, but in most cases you'll get better and more long-lasting results if you use the "Show Me How, Then Let Me Do It" method. Here's how it works.

Using the appropriate survival book as a guideline:
1. Demonstrate how the task should be done by doing it yourself while your child watches.
2. Do the task together or encourage your child to do the task while you watch. (Avoid criticizing and praise anything the child does correctly while you are watching.
3. Let your child do the task alone.
4. Praise the work and express appreciation for what your child has done.

If you'll take a little bit of time to teach your child the skills needed to fulfill your requests, you'll save yourself a lot of energy in the long haul.

So don't just sit there. Do it! And have fun while you're at it. Who knows, doing these nitty-gritty things with your child may give you some of the greatest experiences you'll ever have together — surely some of the most rewarding.

Sincerely,

JOY WILT BERRY

Has your mother or father ever told you to ...

Whenever you are told to clean your room, do you feel overwhelmed and frustrated?

Whenever you are facing a room that you are supposed to clean, do you wonder ...

If any of this sounds familiar to you, you're going to **love** this book!

Because it will tell you exactly where to start and what to do to clean your room. If you follow the instructions outlined in this book, you will be able to clean **any** bedroom, no matter **how** dirty or messy it is!

The first thing you will need to do is ...

1. CLEAR EVERYTHING OFF YOUR BED.

Next ...

2. MAKE YOUR BED.

If your sheets need to be changed, this is the time
to do it. Here's how:

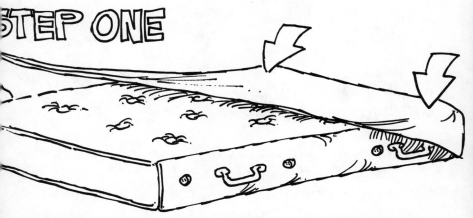

STEP ONE

You'll probably be working with a fitted bottom sheet, and if you are, slip the two top corners of the sheet over the top corners of the mattress.

STEP TWO

Then slip the two bottom corners of the sheet over the bottom corners of the mattress. Lift each mattress corner as you slip the sheet over it.

11

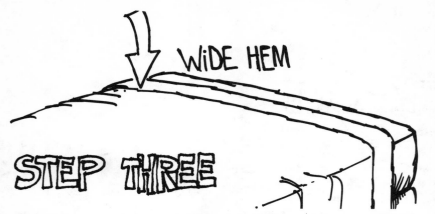

WiDE HEM

STEP THREE

Put the top sheet on the bed, making sure that the side with the wide hem is lined up evenly with the top of the mattress and there is an equal amount of sheet hanging down on both sides of the bed. Also, the "right" or prettiest side of the sheet should be face down on the bed so that it shows when the sheet is pulled back.

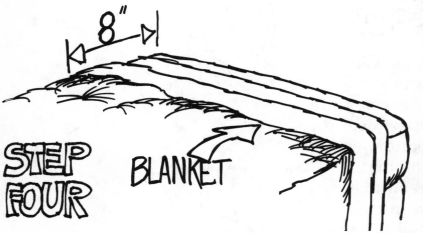

8"

STEP FOUR

BLANKET

Put the blanket (or blankets) on top of the sheet, making sure to put the top edge of the blanket about 8 inches from the top of the mattress. Also be sure to leave an equal amount of blanket hanging down on both sides of the bed.

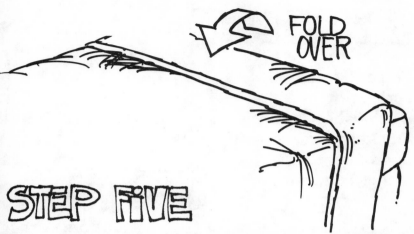

FOLD OVER

STEP FIVE

Now fold the top edge of the sheet over the top edge of the blanket.

STEP SIX

Then tuck the bottom edge of the sheet and blanket under the mattress.

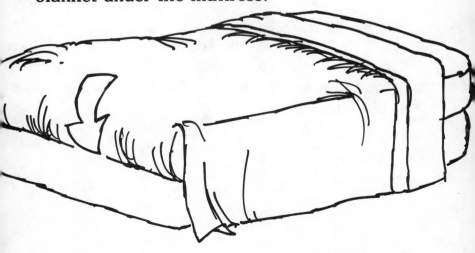

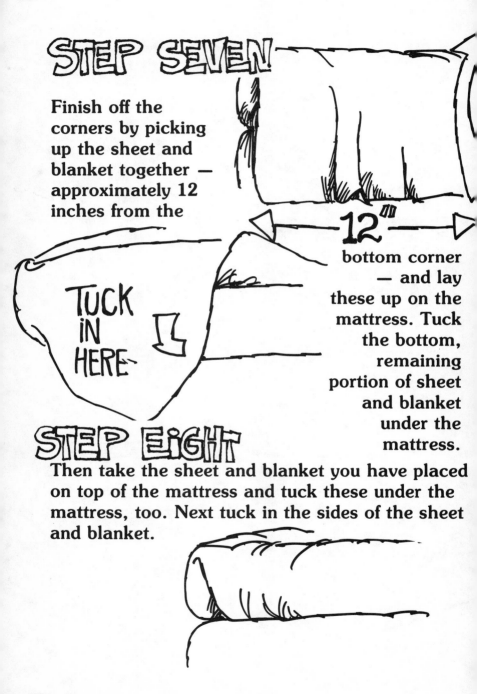

STEP SEVEN

Finish off the corners by picking up the sheet and blanket together — approximately 12 inches from the

12"

bottom corner — and lay these up on the mattress. Tuck the bottom, remaining portion of sheet and blanket under the mattress.

TUCK IN HERE

STEP EIGHT

Then take the sheet and blanket you have placed on top of the mattress and tuck these under the mattress, too. Next tuck in the sides of the sheet and blanket.

STEP NINE

FOLD BACK 20"

To finish making your bed, put your bedspread on the bed while making sure that the sides and bottom edge of the spread barely touch the floor. The top edge should be folded back about 20 inches.

STEP TEN

Put your pillow at the top of the mattress in the middle of the bed along the folded bedspread. Then pull the spread up over the pillow.

PILLOW

After your bed is made ...

3. PICK UP ANYTHING THAT IS OUT OF PLACE AND PUT IT ON YOUR BED.

To make sure you get everything, begin with the area to the left side of your bedroom door and work around the entire room.

Now it is time to ...

4. PUT THE OBJECTS THAT ARE ON YOUR BED AWAY.

Pick up each object one at a time. Decide what to do with it, and then do it. Once you have picked something up, put it away. Do not set it back down.

If you pick up an article of **dirty clothing,** put it (along with all of the other dirty clothes you find) in a pile outside your bedroom door.

If you pick up something that needs to be thrown out, put it in a large paper bag along with all of the other trash you find.

If you pick up something that needs to be put away, don't stuff it "any-old-place" just to get it out of sight.

Put everything away carefully, exactly where it belongs.

If you pick up a clean article of clothing, put it away carefully.

Blouses, shirts, jackets, and dresses should hang on a hanger the same way they hang on your shoulders, with the top button buttoned or the zipper zipped.

Skirts should hang on skirt hangers, or they can be pinned on wire hangers with safety pins.

Pants should be smoothed out, with a crease running down the middle of each leg, then hung by the cuffs on a pants hanger or draped over the bottom of a hanger with an equal amount of the pants hanging on each side of the hanger.

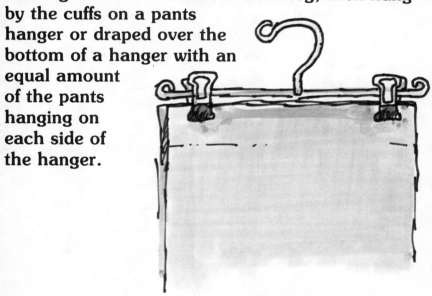

A closet looks neater when all of the skirts or blouses hang together, the pants or skirts hang together, the jackets hang together, etc. **23**

If an article of clothing needs to be folded before it is put away, do it properly.

To fold underwear and shorts, smooth them out and fold them over in half.

Socks should be matched, and then folded in half or thirds. Don't pull the top down over the folded socks because that stretches the top of the socks, and they won't stay up when you wear them.

Belts should be rolled up or hung up.

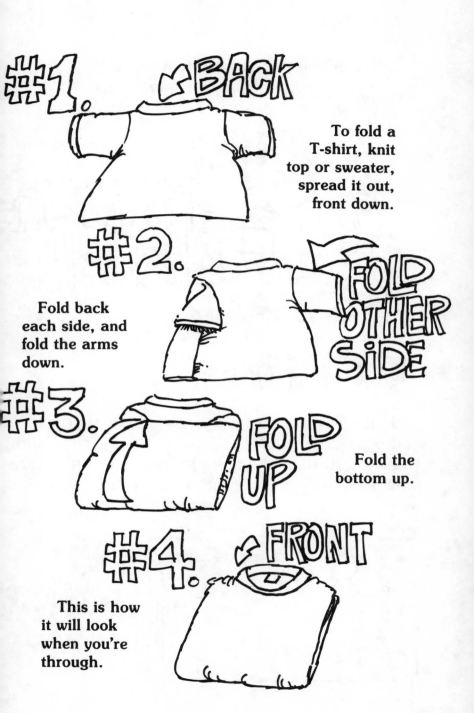

#1. BACK

To fold a
T-shirt, knit
top or sweater,
spread it out,
front down.

#2. FOLD OTHER SIDE

Fold back
each side, and
fold the arms
down.

#3. FOLD UP

Fold the
bottom up.

#4. FRONT

This is how
it will look
when you're
through.

After everything is put away ...

5. DUST THE FURNITURE IN YOUR ROOM.

Begin with the area to the left side of your bedroom door, and work around the entire room. Use a cloth that has a slight amount of furniture polish all over it so that the dust will be picked up and not merely pushed around.

When you dust anything, first dust the top of the object, then the sides, and then the bottoms.

When you have finished dusting the furniture ...

6. VACUUM, SWEEP, OR DUST MOP YOUR ROOM.

Again you should begin with the area to the left of your bedroom door and work your way around the room.

Whenever you vacuum, sweep, or dust mop, make sure you get under and behind your bed and furniture.

By now things should be looking pretty good, but you're not quite finished ...

To completely finish the job you'll need to:

- put the dust rag and vacuum cleaner, broom, or mop away.

- take the dirty clothes pile to wherever the dirty laundry is kept.

- put the trash bag, along with its contents, in the trash can.

If you had a rough time deciding what to do with the things on your bed, you may need to get your room **organized** so that **everything has a place.**

If you decide to organize your things, be sure to:

1. BEGIN WITH A CLEAN ROOM.

If you begin with a disorderly room, you'll only make a bigger mess when you empty out your shelves and drawers. This will most likely frustrate you and make you want to quit before the job is done.

2. WORK ON ONE SMALL AREA AT A TIME.

If you empty every shelf and drawer out at the same time, you'll create a mess that will be overwhelming, and you may end up doing a sloppy job just to get it done.

To help you organize your room ...

1. GET THREE LARGE BOXES (ones that can be closed).

   Label one box "TOSS."

   Label the second box "RECYCLE."

   Label the third box "HOLD."

2. GATHER TOGETHER SOME ITEMS TO STORE THINGS IN.

Here are some items you are going to need:

- several shoe or cigar boxes (these can be gotten from a shoe store). Covered cans work well, too.

- larger cardboard boxes, preferably ones that have lids (these can be gotten from a grocery store).

- plastic storage bags (these can be purchased at a grocery store).

3. DECIDE WHERE YOU ARE GOING TO PUT THINGS.

If you are like most kids, you will need to choose a special shelf, drawer, or area for each of these groups of things:

- books/magazines/comic books, etc.
- art/craft materials
- stationery supplies (for example, papers, pencils, erasers)
- hobbies/collections
- toys/games
- equipment (for sports, bikes, etc.)
- music and musical instruments
- clothes that need to be hung
- shoes/boots, etc.
- personal supplies (combs, brushes, perfume, etc.)
- mementoes (for example, photographs, remembrances, keepsakes)

4. PUT ALL OF THE CONTENTS OF ONE SHELF, DRAWER, OR CLOSET ON YOUR BED.

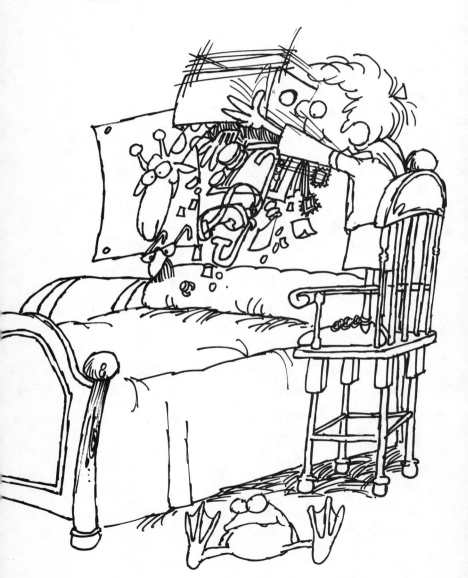

5. PUT THE OBJECTS THAT ARE ON YOUR BED AWAY.

Pick up each object one at a time. Decide what to do with the object, and then do it. Once you have picked something up, put it away. Do not set it back down.

If you pick up an article and decide that it is of no use to anyone (this means that it is completely "used up" or "destroyed"), put it in the box marked "TOSS."

If you pick up an article that is in good/workable condition, but you do not want it anymore, put it in the box marked "RECYCLE."

If you pick up an article that you are not sure about (for example, one that you haven't used for a long time, but one that you are not sure you want to get rid of), put it in the "HOLD" box.

If you pick up an article that you are currently using and want to keep, put it away carefully in the special place you have chosen for it.

Here are a few "tips to remember as you put things away":

- anything that is smaller than a ping pong ball (for example, game parts, barbie doll accessories, pieces to models) should be stored in a plastic storage bag.

- anything that is about the size of a baseball should be stored along with other items about the same size, in shoe or cigar boxes, covered cans, etc.

- if there is no room in your drawers or closets to store your "groups," store all the things in one group together in a box.

- label your drawers, shelves, boxes, etc., so that anyone who puts your things away will put them in the right spot.

- label your things, so that if they're ever misplaced they can be returned to you.

- get rid of worn out or outgrown things before you put any new ones away so you won't have to dig through a pile of old things to get to the new ones.

In regard to your clothes —

- Group your clothes according to a plan. You may want to put all your shirts or blouses together, all your pants together, and so on, or you may want to put all your play clothes together and all your good clothes together. Any plan you decide to use will help you find things more easily and will remind you what has and has not been worn.

- Put your freshly washed clothes on the bottom of the stack and then use the clothes on the top of the stack. This way, everything will be used and you won't end up wearing the same old thing over and over again.

After all of your shelves are organized ...

6. PUT THE LARGE BOX MARKED "TOSS" AND ITS CONTENTS IN THE TRASH.

7. STORE THE BOX MARKED "HOLD."

Write the date on the "HOLD" box, then close it up and put it in a safe place. If after a year you have not "missed" the things in the box, chances are you don't need them. At this point, you should put them in the "RECYCLE" box the next time you organize your room.

8. GET RID OF THE THINGS IN THE "RECYCLE" BOX.

The things in your "RECYCLE" box can be ...
- given to a friend.
- traded for something else.
- sold.
- given to an organization that recycles used things.

Anything still in the box after one week should be gotten rid of immediately, so that it does not get mixed up with your "good" things.

Once your room is organized, it'll be easier to keep it that way if you ...

- put a wastebasket in your room for your trash.
- put a dirty clothes hamper in your room for your dirty clothes.
- straighten up your room every day.
- clean your room at least once a week.
- completely organize your things at least twice a year.

THE END of messy rooms that cause unhappy parents and frustrated kids!